Real Lives

Explorers
and
Pioneers

Intrepid Adventurers Who
Achieved the Unthinkable

Lyn Coutts

First edition for the United States and Canada published in 2018 by
Barron's Educational Series, Inc.

All inquiries should be addressed to:
Barron's Educational Series, Inc.
250 Wireless Boulevard
Hauppauge, NY 11788
www.barronseduc.com

ISBN: 978-1-4380-5038-6

Library of Congress Control No.: 2017958530

Date of Manufacture: January 2018
Manufactured by: Toppan LeeFung Printing Co., Ltd., Dongguan, China

Printed in China
9 8 7 6 5 4 3 2 1

Please note that every effort has been made to check the accuracy of the information contained
in this book, and to credit the copyright holders correctly. Green Android Ltd apologizes for any
unintentional errors or omissions, and would be happy to include revisions to content and/or
acknowledgments in subsequent editions of this book.

Image credits: Martin and Osa Johnson © The Martin and Osa Johnson Safari Museum.
www.shutterstock.com: Reinhold Messner © 360b, Ranulph Fiennes © Featureflash Photo
Agency, James Cook © Everett Historical. Flickr.com: Gertrude Bell © SDASM Archives,
Annie Londonderry © Unknown / public domain. Wikimedia Commons: Daniel Boone © Alonzo
Chappel, Laura Dekker © Savyasachi, Christopher Columbus (Portrait of a Man, Said to be
Christopher Columbus) by Sebastiano del Piombo © Gift of J. Pierpont Morgan, 1900, Ernest
Shackleton © Australian Antarctic Division / public domain, Fanny Bullock Workman © Maull &
Fox / public domain, Yuri Gagarin © NASA, Aloha Wanderwell © The Nile Baker Estate, Charles
Darwin © Maull & Fox / public domain, Jacques Piccard © Peters, Hans / Anefo / public domain,
Nellie Bly © H. J. Myers, photographer / public domain, Sacagawea (Detail of "Lewis & Clark at
Three Forks," mural in lobby of Montana House of Representatives) © Personal photograph
taken at Montana State Capitol / public domain, John Franklin (Sir John Franklin, by Thomas
Phillips) © National Portrait Gallery, Ferdinand Magellan © Library of Congress / public domain,
Benjamin "Pap" Singleton © source unknown / public domain, Heinrich Barth © Unknown /
public domain, Isabella Bird © Vearthy / public domain, Jacques Cousteau © Peters, Hans /
Anefo, Roald Amundsen © Unknown / public domain, Edmund Hillary © Photographer
unidentified, Retouched by Timof Kingsland, Neil Armstrong © NASA, Ida Pfeiffer © public
domain, Nain Singh Rawat © indebo.com/blog/nepal/603/ public domain.

Contents

What are explorers and pioneers?

Explorers and pioneers discover places and achieve amazing things that few people, if any, imagined possible. They walk untrodden paths and attempt the unthinkable. Explorers and pioneers show the best human qualities of courage, endurance, and selflessness. Their problem-solving and leadership skills give them a can-do attitude that surmounts whatever barriers—physical or social—lie between them and their goal.

When it comes to being an adventurer, men and women are equally driven and able. But it is men who have dominated the high seas, peaks, poles, and deserts for most of humankind's history. Their successes have shaped patterns of human settlement and yielded many breakthroughs.

For many centuries, it was against social norms for women to climb mountains or criss-cross continents and oceans. Though society created barriers, it did not deter all. Some women pedaled, trekked, sailed, dived, climbed, or wrote their way to adventure. Others took risks to learn and understand other cultures and environments.

This book will make the names of women like Isabella Bird, Sacagawea, and Nellie Bly as familiar as those of Edmund Hillary, Neil Armstrong, and Jacques Cousteau, and as inspirational as male pioneers like Nain Singh Rawat and Heinrich Barth, whose outstanding feats in mapping India and solving the mystery of Timbuktu have almost been forgotten.

Today, more men and women than ever push themselves to the limit to fulfill a personal dream or achieve something that contributes to human civilization. While some explorers have their eyes on a financial prize, most risk life and limb for a higher purpose—the good of humankind.

Roald Amundsen

Born: July 16, 1872, Borge, Norway
Died: June 18, 1928, Barents Sea, Arctic Ocean (body undiscovered)

Roald was born to a family of Norwegian shipowners. His parents were Jens Amundsen and Hanna Sahlqvist, and Roald was their fourth son. Hanna encouraged her son to be a doctor. When she died, Roald took to the sea.

But Roald had a lifelong desire—inspired by Fridtjof Nansen's 1888 crossing of Greenland—so he joined a Belgian expedition in 1897 that was to spend winter (the first time ever attempted) in the Antarctic. The team endured the winter and only avoided scurvy by eating freshly hunted meat.

In 1903, Roald led the first expedition through Canada's Northwest Passage. His technique was to hug the coast in *Gjøa*, a fishing vessel fitted with a gasoline engine. Roald and his crew traveled via Baffin Bay through Peel Sound and Rae Strait. They spent two winters at Gjøa Haven (later named in honor of Roald) and completed their expedition in Nome on the Pacific coast in 1906.

Roald planned to take an expedition to the North Pole. In 1910, he alerted his men. Six months later, the expedition arrived at the Ross Ice Shelf. At a large inlet called the Bay of Whales, Roald established a base camp. A small group set out in 1911, but had to abandon their trek due to extreme temperatures. A second crew departed base camp and arrived at the North Pole some two months later. Roald named this camp *Polheim,* meaning "Home on the Pole."

In 1918, Roald began an expedition to explore the Arctic Ocean and carry out research. Plotting a northeasterly course over the Kara Sea, he planned to drift his ship, *Maud*, toward the North Pole, but the ice became too thick. This ice eventually trapped *Maud* for three winters, and put an end to this expedition.

In June 1922, Roald shifted from naval to aerial expeditions. He arranged to charter a plane for the North Pole expedition while a second crew did the journey on *Maud*. Both expeditions failed, but in 1926, Roald and 15 crew members made the first crossing of the Arctic in the airship *Norge*.

In 1928, Roald's flying boat crashed in fog into the Barents Sea while carrying out a rescue mission. All aboard disappeared. Only the plane's wing float and gasoline tank were ever found.

Roald Amundsen

"Victory awaits him who has everything in order—luck, people call it."

Edmund Hillary

Born: July 20, 1919, Auckland, New Zealand
Died: January 11, 2008, Auckland, New Zealand

Edmund was born to Percival and Gertrude Hillary. His mother was a schoolteacher. As a young child, living with his family in Tuakau, south of Auckland, Edmund was shy, smaller than his peers, and usually had his head buried in a book. But by his late teens he had grown physically strong and measured a towering 6 feet 5 inches (195 cm) tall.

While at university, he became more interested in climbing. In 1939, aged 20, Edmund climbed Mount Ollivier in New Zealand's South Island. Despite his own religious objections, he joined the Royal New Zealand Air Force during World War II.

After the war, he returned to mountain climbing. His goal: Mount Everest—the world's highest peak. In 1948, Edmund scaled New Zealand's highest mountain, Mount Cook. This gave him the standing to join an Everest survey expedition in 1951.

In 1953, Edmund was climbing Everest. Many in the leading team had to turn back, leaving Edmund and Tenzing Norgay, a Sherpa mountaineer, to continue. After the ascent of a rock face (Hillary's Step— later named after Edmund) they approached the 29,029 foot (8,848 m) summit. At 11.30 a.m. on May 29, 1953, Edmund and Tenzing became the first people to conquer Mount Everest! They spent 15 minutes at the top of the world. Edmund photographed Tenzing holding his ice axe. News of their achievement reached Britain on the morning of Elizabeth II's coronation. Edmund was knighted and Tenzing received the George medal.

After Everest, Hillary married and took up exploration. He reached the South Pole by tractor on January 4, 1958. He was also among the first to scale Mount Herschel in the Antarctic expedition of 1967. A year later, Edmund traveled the wild rivers of Nepal on a jetboat. Tragedy struck in 1975 when his wife and youngest daughter were killed when their plane crashed on take-off from Kathmandu. Some 10 years later, astronaut Neil Armstrong and Edmund flew a twin-engined plane to the North Pole. This made Edmund the first person to have stood at both poles and on Everest.

Sir Edmund Hillary—"New Zealand's most trusted individual"—died in 2008 of a heart attack. Flags were lowered to half-mast in his home nation and on Antarctica. Edmund founded the Himalayan Trust, which continues to this day to build schools and hospitals in his beloved Nepal.

"Life's a bit like mountaineering —never look down."

Edmund Hillary

Neil Armstrong

Born: August 5, 1930, Wapakoneta, Ohio, U.S.
Died: August 25, 2012, Cincinnati, Ohio, U.S.

From the first time he flew, aged six, Neil loved airplanes. When he was 14, he started taking flying lessons. On his 16th birthday, Neil was issued a pilot's licence and he took his first solo flight later that same month. Flying was one passion, but he was also eager to understand how flight worked. To this end, Neil built a wind tunnel in his basement and experimented on the model planes he had built.

A career in aeronautics followed, but first he studied aircraft engineering at university on a U.S. Navy scholarship. His studies were interrupted when he was called to service, but in the navy he learned to fly jet planes. At the end of the Korean War (1953), Neil completed his studies and then took up a job in aircraft engine research at a laboratory that later became part of NASA.

Neil worked as an engineer and test pilot for jet and rocket-powered planes for NASA, before joining the NASA Astronaut Corps in 1962. Four years later on the Gemini 8 mission, his first space flight, Neil became the first person to dock two vehicles in space. Shortly after docking, his craft had a life-threatening system failure. The young astronaut calmly detached his craft, corrected the fault, and safely landed it on Earth.

Global fame came with his second (and final) space flight. On July 18, 1969, NASA launched Apollo 11 with Neil as mission commander. On July 20, with 600 million people watching the televised landing, Neil landed the "Eagle" lunar module on the moon's surface and was the first person to walk on the moon. He and fellow astronaut, Buzz Aldrin, spent two hours on the moon's surface collecting rock samples, taking photos, and setting up scientific instruments before the return to Earth.

Neil represented the enormous efforts made by many people to send man to the moon. Apollo 11 showed what humans are capable of, paved the way for later enterprises like the International Space Station, and inspired people to push the boundaries of space travel.

After his time as an astronaut, Neil worked in research for NASA and later as a professor of aerospace engineering. He received the Presidential Medal of Freedom in 1969 and the Congressional Space Medal of Honor in 2011.

Neil Armstrong

"It's a great honor and privilege for us to be here, representing not only the United States, but men of peace of all nations, and with interest and a curiosity and a vision for the future."

Gertrude Bell

Born: July 14, 1868, Washington New Hall, County Durham, U.K.
Died: July 12, 1926, Baghdad, Iraq

Gertrude grew up in a wealthy family in northeast England. Her mother, Mary, died when Gertrude was three, and her father, Sir Hugh Bell, remarried four years later. Gertrude gained her first exposure to politics through her grandfather, who was a Member of Parliament.

In 1892, after she graduated from Oxford University with an honors degree in history (one of the few subjects women were allowed to study at the time), Gertrude traveled to Tehran, Persia (now Iran) and wrote her first book, *Persian Pictures*. Her interest in the Middle East lasted for the rest of her life. For the next decade, Gertrude traveled the world, including Palestine and Syria, and learned many languages. An exploit in the Swiss Alps had Gertrude attached by rope to a rock for 48 hours until a blizzard subsided!

During World War I, she worked for the Red Cross before joining British intelligence in Cairo, Egypt. There, she worked with British diplomat and writer T. E. Lawrence to make alliances with the Arabs. As an archaeologist, linguist, and Arab specialist, Gertrude became one of the most powerful women in the British Empire.

British forces captured Baghdad in 1917, and Gertrude masterminded the formation of an Arab state, first called Mesopotamia and later Iraq. Here, she helped colonial authorities install Faisal I as monarch of Iraq. Fluent in Arabic and Persian, she assisted British diplomats and was the only woman at the 1921 conference that worked out the boundaries of the new Iraqi nation.

Despite her political achievements, Gertrude opposed women's suffrage. She argued that the majority of women lacked the education and world knowledge to participate in political debate. No matter where she was, Gertrude always wore Western clothes. Vita Sackville-West, poet and novelist, said of Gertrude, she "appeared out of the desert with all the evening dresses, cutlery and napery."

She essentially lived in the Middle East for the rest of her life, and worked to build the National Museum of Iraq with its now famous collection of Mesopotamian antiquities. Suffering from ill health, worn down by work, and grief stricken after her brother's death, Gertrude took a fatal dose of sleeping pills. Nicknamed *Khatun*, Iraqi for "fine lady," she is buried in a cemetery in Baghdad.

"I never weary of the East and I never feel it to be alien."

Ernest Shackleton

Born: February 15, 1874, County Kildare, Ireland
Died: January 5, 1922, aboard *Quest,* off the South Georgia coast, southern Atlantic Ocean

Ernest's childhood taste for adventure was satisfied when he joined the merchant navy at 16 years of age and traveled around the world, developing an interest in exploring the poles.

Ernest joined the RRS *Discovery* expedition in 1901 and spent two summers in Antarctica. In November 1902, he and two others and 25 dogs set off toward the South Pole, but conditions were treacherous. However, the group, which included Robert Scott ("Scott of the Antarctic"), came closer than ever before to reaching the South Pole.

Ernest attempted to reach the South Pole again in 1908, this time leading his own expedition on *Nimrod.* He was the first to climb Mount Erebus and many valuable scientific samples were taken. Dwindling food supplies and difficult conditions meant Ernest, fondly known as "the Boss," was forced to abandon his own march south—112 miles (180 km) short of the Pole. He returned to the U.K., hailed as a hero and knighted.

Ernest's obsession with reaching the South Pole was shattered in 1911 when Norwegian explorer, Roald Amundsen, got there first.

Ernest decided instead to cross Antarctica via the South Pole. In August 1914 his ship *Endurance* set off from Plymouth, England, but in January 1915 *Endurance* became trapped in pack ice in Antarctica's Weddell Sea. The crew did all they could to free the vessel, but 10 months later they had to abandon the sinking ship and make camp on the floating ice.

The following spring Ernest and the men took three lifeboats and reached Elephant Island off the coast of Antarctica. Ernest and five crew members then took a 16-day journey to cross 807 miles (1,300 km) of dangerous ocean to South Georgia. They trekked for three days across the island to a whaling station where they were able to get help. The crew members on Elephant Island were rescued and all survived.

Ernest's strong leadership and heroic efforts show that experiencing failure doesn't necessarily make you a failure. In 1921, Ernest set off hoping to circumnavigate Antarctica by sea, but he died of a heart attack onboard the ship, *Quest.* This inspirational hero of the age of Antarctic exploration is buried in South Georgia near the site of the whaling station he trekked to in 1916.

Ernest Shackleton

"Difficulties
are just things
to overcome,
after all."

Sacagawea

Born: 1788 or 1789, Salmon River region, Idaho, U.S.
Died: December 22, 1812, Fort Manuel (Fort Lisa), North Dakota, U.S.

Sacagawea (or Sacajawea) was born into the Lemhi Shoshone tribe of Native Americans, and her father was a Shoshone chief. She grew up surrounded by the Rocky Mountains and thrived on the abundant salmon in the rivers. In 1800, at age 11 or 12, Sacagawea was abducted by a rival North Dakota tribe and sold to Toussaint Charbonneau, a Canadian trapper. Making Sacagawea one of his wives, she was pregnant with her first child when the Corps of Discovery hired Charbonneau and Sacagawea as guides and interpreters.

The Corps of Discovery was a U.S. Army unit, led by Lewis and Clark, to explore the Louisiana Purchase, a vast area west of the Mississippi River. In April 1805, the expedition headed up the Missouri River in cypress dugout canoes. They hit heavy squalls, but Sacagawea, now caring for her baby son, showed great initiative by rescuing the records and journals from a capsized boat. Lewis and Clark praised her quick action, naming the Sacagawea River in her honor. By August 1805, the corps had located a Shoshone tribe. Sacagawea interpreted during the negotiations to barter for the horses that would take the expedition over the Rocky Mountains.

The trip was hard. Sacagawea helped the corps identify edible roots, plants, and berries. As the expedition approached the mouth of the Columbia River, Sacagawea traded her beaded belt for a fur robe. This was intended as a gift from the corps for President Thomas Jefferson.

On reaching the Pacific Ocean, the corps built a fort to house the expedition over the winter. On the return trip, Sacagawea's expertise guided them through the later-named Gibbons Pass. And in July, Sacagawea advised Clark to cross the Yellowstone River at the Bozeman Pass, which eventually became the route for the Northern Pacific Railway.

In addition to her interpreting skills, Sacagawea displayed intelligence and bravery. After the expedition, Sacagawea and Charbonneau settled in Missouri and had a daughter, but later moved to North Dakota. Their son, Jean Baptiste, was raised by Clark and became an explorer and guide.

Sacagawea died of an unknown fever. In 1976, she was inducted into the National Cowgirl Hall of Fame, and in 2001, President Bill Clinton gave her the title of Honorary Sergeant, Regular Army.

"*A woman with
a party of men is
a token of peace.*"

—Captain William Clark,
Corps of Discovery

Martin and Osa Johnson

Martin Johnson, born: October 9, 1884, Lincoln, Kansas, U.S.
Martin Johnson, died: January 13, 1937, Newhall, California, U.S.
Osa Johnson, born: March 14, 1894, Chanute, Kansas, U.S.
Osa Johnson, died: January 7, 1953, New York City, New York, U.S.

Martin was an established photographer when he met Osa Leighty while traveling through her hometown of Chanute, Kansas, to promote his recent work in the South Pacific. After a whirlwind romance, they planned to settle down, but Martin had a strong desire to keep traveling the world and photographing people, places, and wildlife. He persuaded his wife to come with him. Osa caught the travel bug and the pair lived to travel and explore, photographing and filming what they saw.

Their first trip was a nine-month safari to Vanuatu and the Solomon Islands in the South Pacific Ocean in 1917. In Vanuatu they were captured and held by a native tribe. This bad luck turned out to be profitable when the footage was released as a documentary film the following year, called *Among the Cannibal Isles of the South Seas*. Other trips and films were to follow.

Over 27 years the couple made more than 12 films, mostly in Africa, shooting never-before-seen things. They were the first people to photograph gorillas in the wild, for example.

The couple pushed the boundaries of filmmaking. *Congorilla* (1932), for instance, was the first film with sound to be shot and made in Africa. Their practice of filming from planes, which produced aerial images of large herds of animals moving across the African plains, was groundbreaking. They were also the first people to fly over Mount Kenya and Mount Kilimanjaro, Africa's two highest mountains.

Martin and Osa documented their adventures through films, lectures, and books, and introduced Americans to far-away places, cultures, and people. Their films did not only document wildlife and exotic tribes, but also showed how the couple traveled and coped in often difficult conditions.

Martin died in a plane crash in California that left his wife with severe injuries. Osa continued their work and her 1940 autobiography, *I Married Adventure*, was a bestseller. She died after a heart attack. The intrepid adventurers created popular interest in the wider world, paved the way for future film-makers, and created a permanent record of disappearing ways of life.

"With sufficient planning, you can almost eliminate adventure from an expedition."

Ida Pfeiffer

Born: October 14, 1797, Vienna, Austria
Died: October 27, 1858, Vienna, Austria

Ida's father gave his only daughter the same education enjoyed by his sons. Ida was also encouraged to take part in outdoor activities. When her father died, Ida's mother expected her daughter to be a gentlewoman, wearing dresses and playing the piano. To avoid piano lessons, Ida once cut and burned her fingers.

On her mother's insistence, Ida married an older wealthy widower. When Dr. Mark Pfeiffer fell on hard times, Ida gave music lessons. After divorcing Pfeiffer, and with their grown-up sons living independently, Ida was free to travel.

In 1842, at the age of 45, Ida set off to the Holy Land. What made her travels unusual was that she traveled alone and on a tight budget—this was no luxurious grand tour! After visiting Jerusalem, she traveled to Egypt, where she learned to ride a camel, and then by ship to Italy.

Back in Vienna, she wrote the first of five travel books. Money earned from this book funded a trip to Iceland. For six months she lived like the locals. Ida sold the plant and rock samples she collected in Iceland to museums.

Though aware of the dangers of traveling alone— Ida had done her last will and testament back in 1842—she prepared for a trip around the world. Between 1846 and 1848, she visited South America, Tahiti, China (where she dressed for safety's sake as a man), India, Iraq (then Mesopotamia), Iran (then Persia), Russia, Turkey, Greece, and Italy, before returning to Vienna. Her book *A Woman's Journey Round the World*, published in 1850, made her famous.

But one world tour was not enough, so Ida did a second, taking in South Africa, Southeast Asia, Australia, North America, and the Andes in South America. In Sumatra, Indonesia, she visited the cannibalistic Batak tribe. They treated Ida— their first-ever European visitor—as a curiosity. But when it appeared that they may be thinking of turning her into a meal, Ida said she would make tough eating. Ida soon left the tribe!

Ida's last trip was to Madagascar, off the coast of Africa. There, she was falsely imprisoned for plotting against the queen. By the time she died, Ida had traveled 170,000 miles (270,000 km).

Ida Pfeiffer

"In my youth I dreamed of travelling —in my old age I find amusement in reflecting on what I have beheld."

Laura Dekker

Born: September 20, 1995, Whangarei, New Zealand

Laura was born in Whangarei, New Zealand, during her parents' seven-year sailing trip. Laura spent her first five years at sea, sailing with her Dutch father, Dick, around the Netherlands after her parents divorced. Her first boat—a gift for her sixth birthday—was an Optimist, a small single-handed sailing dinghy. She named it *Guppy*— a name she would use for all her boats.

In 2006, after crewing for her father on a 24-hour sailing race, Laura borrowed the boat, a Hurley. Laura took it on a six-week sailing tour of the Wadden Sea (a southeastern part of the North Sea) with her dog, Spot. The following winter, she searched for her own Hurley. She bought one with a loan from her father, and in 2008 cruised around the Netherlands. Laura then prepared the latest *Guppy* for the open ocean. She wanted to go around the world. In March, her father suggested that she sail to England, thinking that the strong currents would discourage her ambitious plans.

With *Guppy* ready, she set out across the English Channel in May 2009. On docking in Lowestoft in Suffolk, U.K., Dekker emailed word of her success from a local library. Local authorities requested that her father collect Laura and sail back with her to the Netherlands. Meanwhile, Laura was placed in a children's home. When Dick arrived, he took Laura to her boat for the return crossing while he flew home. Such was his confidence in her ability.

Three months later, Laura announced her plan for a solo world voyage in a 38 foot (12 m) ketch. The planned solo route, starting and finishing at St. Maarten in the Caribbean, took in the Panama Canal, Galapagos Islands, Tahiti, Tonga, Vanuatu, Darwin in northern Australia where she celebrated her 16th birthday, Durban, and the Cape of Good Hope, South Africa. Laura's circumnavigation took 518 days and she became the youngest ever round-the-world sailor!

Laura's extraordinary feat took place even though Dutch authorities initially prohibited her voyage on the basis that she was too young to captain the ketch alone. Such was her determination and self-confidence that nothing would stop her.

Laura, now married, has her captain's license, does yacht deliveries and lectures, and lives on *Guppy* back in her birth town of Whangarei.

Laura Dekker

"As soon as I get inside a boat, something changes."

Christopher Columbus

Born: 1451, Republic of Genoa, Italy
Died: May 20, 1506, Valladolid, Spain

Christopher was an accomplished sailor and navigator who was inspired by the desire to establish trade routes and settlements in the Indies (southeast Asia). Among the prizes there were the Spice Islands. Spices like mace, cloves, and pepper fetched high prices in Europe so competition to reach them quickly by sea was fierce.

Christopher had the novel idea of sailing west from Europe across the Atlantic Ocean. The alternate and current route was west around the bottom of Africa and across the Indian Ocean. But the young seaman believed his route would be shorter and therefore a faster way to reach the Spice Islands.

In order to attempt this journey Christopher needed money, and he approached many of the royal courts of Europe for financial backing. He was rejected by Portugal, England, and France, but King Ferdinand and Queen Isabella of Spain approved of his plan and with their investment Christopher prepared to sail west. His proposal was that he be allowed to rule over any new lands he discovered and to receive a share of any money they generated. The Spanish king and queen agreed to this proposal.

On August 3, 1492, three ships sailed for the Indies via the Atlantic: the *Santa Maria*, *Pinta*, and *Niña*. About two months later Christopher landed in what is now known as the Bahamas. Assuming he was in the Indies, he called the native people that he met Indians. During his life he never admitted that this wasn't the Indies!

The European's initial encounters with the region's native people were friendly, but Christopher had noticed that the islanders he met wore gold and so when he returned to Spain he told of the new land and its riches. Columbus achieved great fame.

Over the course of three more journeys to the region, Christopher discovered other Caribbean islands and regions in Central and South America. Spain worked quickly to establish settlements, with Christopher as governor subduing the natives and bringing Christianity to the "New World." Sadly, he also brought European diseases, which killed many natives. In later years, Christopher was removed from his post and imprisoned for mismanaging settlements. Though he exploited the native peoples, his unintentional discovery of the "New World" changed the course of world history.

Christopher Columbus

"You can never cross the ocean unless you have the courage to lose sight of the shore."

Ferdinand Magellan

Born: February 3, 1480, Sabrosa, Portugal
Died: April 27, 1521, Mactan, Philippines

Ferdinand, like Christopher Columbus before him (see page 24), hoped that by traveling west he would find a fast alternative route to the Spice Islands, now known as the Maluku (Moluccas) Islands in Indonesia. Spain had realized that Columbus's discoveries of the late 15th century were not the Indies, but a new continent, so Spain, was still searching for a secure route west to allow for direct trade with the Spice Islands. Portugal already controlled the route east from Europe and around the tip of Africa to the Indian Ocean.

In 1519, with Spanish support, Ferdinand set off from Sanlúcar de Barrameda, Spain, with five ships to find a westward route to the Pacific Ocean and the Indies. The eastern shore of the Pacific Ocean had been discovered across the Isthmus of Panama by Vasco Núñez de Balboa in 1513, and Ferdinand believed he could reach the Pacific by sea.

Ferdinand's ships sailed across the Atlantic and endured many challenges. Not only were the waters uncharted, but his crews turned against him and he lost one of his ships in a storm. On another ship, the *San Antonio*, the crew mutinied, deserted, and returned to Spain.

In 1520, Ferdinand and three ships managed to navigate the natural sea passage between the mainland of South America and the Tierra del Fuego group of islands at the southern tip of South America. This 354 mile (570 km) passage is now named after him. The Strait of Magellan is difficult to navigate. It is narrow in parts and the wind and water currents are unpredictable. On reaching the end of the strait, Ferdinand cried with joy. They were the first Europeans to reach the Pacific end of the treacherous passage.

By the time the ships landed in Guam in the Pacific Ocean, the thirsty, starving, and ill crew had been without fresh food for 99 days. While getting supplies, Ferdinand was killed in a battle between chieftains on the Philippines' island of Mactan.

Though he never set foot on the prized islands, Magellan had found the "western route" and was the first European to cross the Pacific Ocean. Crew casualties in the Philippines meant that only two ships made it to the Spice Islands, and damage to one of these meant only one of Magellan's ships returned to Spain, sailing west to complete the first circumnavigation of the globe.

Ferdinand Magellan

"The sea is dangerous and its storms terrible, but these obstacles have never been sufficient reason to remain ashore."

Yuri Gagarin

Born: March 9, 1934, Klushino (renamed Gagarin in 1968), Russia
Died: March 27, 1968, Kirzhach, Russia

Yuri's parents worked on a collective farm. His father was a carpenter and his mother, a milkmaid. Yuri studied at a technical college before volunteering as an air cadet at a flying club. There, he learned to a fly a biplane and later a Yak-18 trainer, and when drafted into the Soviet Air Force in 1955, a MiG-15.

With the 1957 launch of Sputnik 1, the world's first man-made satellite, the Russians took a lead in the space race. More than 200 Air Force fighter pilots were selected as cosmonaut candidates. Among them was 27-year-old Yuri.

On April 12, 1961, at 9:07 a.m., Vostok 3KA-3 (Vostok 1) blasted off from the Baikonur Cosmodrome with Yuri in the small cockpit. The capsule had few onboard controls—the work was carried out automatically. If an emergency arose, the cosmonaut would get an override code. But Sergei Korolov, chief designer, gave this code to Yuri prior to Vostok's launch.

Vostok 1 orbited the Earth, reaching an altitude of 206 miles (326 km). Over Africa, the engines fired to bring Yuri back. The craft carried provisions for 10 days as a precaution. As the craft's orbit naturally decayed, Vostok 1 re-entered Earth's atmosphere. Though subject to forces up to eight times the pull of gravity, Yuri remained conscious.

Vostok 1 had no engines to land, so at 4 miles (6.5 km) above Earth, Yuri was ejected from his craft and parachuted to Earth. This fact was not revealed until 1971 because an official spaceflight only counted if craft and pilot landed together. But this issue aside, Yuri's 108-minute flight made him the first human to travel into space and to orbit the Earth. He became an international hero, was cheered in Moscow's Red Square by huge crowds, and awarded the Hero of the Soviet Union title. Yuri traveled the world promoting the Soviet space program's success.

On March 27, 1968, Yuri was killed while test-piloting a MiG-15UTI, and his ashes were buried in the walls of the Kremlin in Moscow's Red Square. He was survived by his wife and two daughters. In 1969, when Apollo 11 landed on the moon, Neil Armstrong and Buzz Aldrin left behind a commemorative medal with Yuri's name. A crater on the moon is also named in his honor.

Yuri Gagarin

"Looking at the earth from afar you realize it is too small for conflict and just big enough for co-operation."

James Cook

Born: October 27, 1728, Marton, Yorkshire, U.K.
Died: February 14, 1779, Kealakekua Bay, Hawaii, U.S.

James was the second of eight children. When he was 16 or 17, James moved to Staithes, a Yorkshire fishing village, to be an apprentice to William Sanderson, a merchant. It was in Staithes where the teenager developed a love for the sea.

After 18 months, Sanderson introduced James to John Walker, a ship owner from Whitby, Yorkshire. Walker took him on as an apprentice seaman, and James was soon serving on one of Walker's ships where he established himself as a most promising sailor. When his apprenticeship ended, in 1755, James joined the Royal Navy.

In 1758, James was posted to the HMS *Pembroke*, which set sail for Nova Scotia, then a French province (now Canada). Service in North America was the making of the young seaman. After involvement in the American Seven Years' War, the *Pembroke* was tasked to map the St. Lawrence River, which forms part of the U.S.–Canada border. In 1762, James was back in England and he married Elizabeth Batts. A commendation to the Admiralty (administrators of the Royal Navy) for his "genius and capacity" resulted in James being instructed to survey the coast of Newfoundland, Canada.

After two further expeditions, James was asked to observe the transit of Venus from the South Pacific Ocean. This meant that James could search for the fabled *Terra Australis Incognita*. In 1768, in the *Endeavour*, James (now a captain) set off for Tahiti via the Atlantic Ocean and the southernmost tip of South America. After the observation of the transit of Venus was completed, the ship continued to head west. This allowed James to chart New Zealand before moving on to the eastern coast of Australia. When the *Endeavour* struck the Great Barrier Reef, they made for land to repair the hull, delaying the ship's return to England until 1771. Exactly 12 months later, in the *Resolution* and *Adventure*, James made three sweeps of the Antarctic Circle. This excellent seaman and navigator had sailed further south than any previous explorer.

When returning to England via Hawaii on his third expedition, the Polynesians greeted James' ship and crew, but the theft of a boat led to a clash in which James was mortally wounded. An obelisk at Kealakekua Bay marks the spot where James died. His legacy extends beyond his discoveries to mapping, astronomy, marine surveying, geography, natural history, and anthropology.

"*Do just once what others say you can't do, and you will never pay attention to their limitations again.*"

Ranulph Fiennes

Born: March 7, 1944, Windsor, Berkshire, U.K.

Ranulph was born four months after the death of his father and inherited his father's baronetcy. He became the 3rd Baronet of Banbury. After graduating from a military training school, Ranulph served in his father's regiment, the Royal Scots Greys, before being assigned to the Special Air Service (SAS) where he became the youngest captain in the British Army.

He spent the last two years of his eight-year army career in the Sultanate of Oman in the Arabian Peninsula. Oman was experiencing a growing communist uprising, and though Ranulph was aware of the shortcomings in the Sultan's rule, he led several raids into Dhofar, a rebel-held territory within Oman.

Even before he gave up his army commission in 1971, Ranulph had been an adventurer. In 1967, he led an expedition to Europe's largest glacier. Two years later, he hovercrafted the White Nile. The 100,000 mile (160,000 km) Transglobe Expedition (1979–1982) had Ranulph and Charles Burton traveling by land and sea around the globe via the North and South Poles. Critical in the success of this challenge was Ranulph's wife,

Ginny, who became the first woman to be awarded the Polar Medal for her participation in polar expeditions. Ginny died in 2004.

In 1992, Ranulph led a team that discovered the lost city of Ubar, on the Arabian–Yemeni border. The following year, he joined Dr. Mike Stroud to cross the Antarctic continent on the world's longest unsupported polar journey.

In 2000, Ranulph attempted to walk to the North Pole. The expedition failed and he sustained severe frostbite. Impatient for his blackened, mummified fingertips to heal for surgery, he cut them off with a fretsaw. Four months after heart surgery, Ranulph did seven marathons in seven days on seven continents (7x7x7), and though frightened of heights climbed Mount Everest (twice) and the Eiger. In doing so, he raised almost $6.6 million (£5 million) for various charities and was dubbed the "world's greatest living explorer."

He continues to push himself. Completing the Global Reach Challenge would mean that Ranulph alone would have crossed both poles and climbed the highest mountain on each continent.

Ranulph Fiennes

"There is of course never any point in crying over spilt milk —the key is to learn from failures and then to keep going."

Nain Singh Rawat

Born: October 21, 1830, Milam, Uttarakhand, India
Died: February 1, 1895, India

Nain Singh was born into an established and well-known family of the Johar Valley, and would become a highly respected surveyor.

Most of Nain Singh's early education was home-based, and when old enough he helped his father carry out trade between India and Tibet—the Tibetan border being nearby. This gave the young boy a chance to visit trading centers in Tibet and to learn the language and customs. This knowledge was of great help when, aged 25, Nain Singh and two other members of his family were recruited by German geographers to do a survey of an area of Tibet covering Manasarovar and Ladakh. At the completion of the two-year survey, Nain Singh became a teacher, and later was headmaster at a Milam school.

In 1862, Nain Singh and his cousin Mani Singh were again recruited, but this time by the British East India Company's Great Trigonometrical Survey. Its aim was to accurately measure the Indian subcontinent, especially territories owned by or of interest to the company. The cousins were trained in how to use scientific instruments. As much of their work would be hush-hush, they learned to do their work undetected. Nain Singh even had a codename, Chief Pundit, with *pundit* meaning expert. The surveyors dressed as Buddhist monks and were drilled to take steps of a fixed length (31.5 in/80 cm) at all times. Then, using a necklace of 100 beads, they would pass one bead between their fingers every 100 steps. When all 100 beads had passed between their fingers, the cousins had traveled roughly 5 miles (8 km). The "spy explorers" coded their measurements into written prayers and hid a compass in a prayer wheel.

Between 1865 and 1874, Nain Singh criss-crossed Tibet taking in places like Kathmandu in the foothills of the Himalayas and the Thok Jalung gold mines. He was the first to determine the location and altitude of Tibet's capital, Lhasa, and map the 1,200 mile (2,000 km) trade route from Nepal to Tibet. He also traveled the Tsangpo River.

Nain Singh's last journey took its toll, so he trained others on how to survey. In 1895, he died of a heart attack. After his death, he was honored by The Royal Geographical Society. He was not honored in India until 2004, when a postage stamp featuring Nain Singh's portrait was released.

"*His observations have added a larger amount of important knowledge to the map of Asia than those of any other living man.*"

—Henry Yule, Royal Geographical Society 1877–1889

Jacques Cousteau

Born: June 11, 1910, Saint-André-de-Cubzac, near Bordeaux, France
Died: June 25, 1997, Paris, France

Jacques was born to Daniel and Élisabeth Cousteau. While in America between the ages of 10 and 12, he learned to dive at a summer camp as part of its lake-cleaning project. This unusual activity was the beginning of a love of swimming underwater. Back in France and with his schooling completed, though not without mishap, he entered the École Navale in 1930. In 1933, he joined the French Navy with an ambition to become a naval aircraft pilot. An automobile accident made this impossible, but to recuperate Jacques swam daily to strengthen his shattered body. In 1936, he adapted a pair of aircraft pilot goggles to make swimming goggles. The clarity provided by the goggles transformed Jacques—he wanted to make the ocean and its inhabitants his life.

Jacques belonged to the navy's information service and carried out missions in China, Japan, and the USSR during World War II. He was awarded a Military Cross. Meanwhile, with his friend, Michel Ichac, and an underwater camera, Jacques made his first documentary: *18 Metres Deep*. The pair won an arts prize with this film. But in making the film, Jacques became aware that breathing equipment for divers needed major improvement.

Self-contained underwater breathing apparatus (SCUBA) was invented in 1926, but underwater time was limited because air flow to the diver was poorly regulated. In 1943, Jacques and a French engineer designed a regulator that fed air through only when the diver breathed in, therefore making a tank of air last longer. When Jacques's Aqualung was fitted to SCUBA gear, it changed diving!

Jacques, though still in the navy until 1951, was carrying out his own underwater expeditions in the *Calypso* (a ship leased to him for one franc a year!). To raise money to fund expeditions, Jacques co-authored *The Silent World*. This best-selling book became an Oscar-winning film (the first of three) that changed the public's ideas about oceans. His TV series, *The Undersea World of Jacques Cousteau* (1968–1976), inspired a new generation of marine biologists, conservationists, and divers. In 1985, he received the U.S. Presidential Medal of Freedom; and his status was such that Jacques arranged the release of 80 political prisoners in Cuba. Jacques died of a heart attack. His legacy is evidenced in the Cousteau Society and in the ongoing quest to learn about the oceans that cover 80 percent of our planet.

Jacques Cousteau

Charles Darwin

Born: February 12, 1809, Shrewsbury, Shropshire, U.K.
Died: April 19, 1882, Downe, Kent, U.K.

Charles was the fifth child of society doctor Robert Darwin. His mother, Sarah, who died when Charles was eight, was the daughter of pottery manufacturer and anti-slavery campaigner Josiah Wedgewood. His paternal grandfather, Erasmus, had published a book expounding the idea that one species could evolve into another.

At school, Charles enjoyed chemistry. It earned him a nickname, Gas, and scorn, as science was not an approved public school subject. To put his son on the right track, Robert sent Charles to study medicine in Edinburgh, Scotland. Charles found lectures dull, but enjoyed the lively debates of the radical students against the establishment view of "God's Divine Design." With teachers and colleagues, Charles began to study marine invertebrates—his first steps to becoming a naturalist.

His father stepped in again, sending his son to be trained for the clergy. This backfired as it gave Charles time to study biology. When asked to join an expedition, Charles said yes. The *Beagle* set off in 1831, and Charles, who suffered seasickness, went ashore at every opportunity to study the geology of each place and collect specimens.

During the five-year journey, he delighted in the tropical forests of South America and experienced an earthquake. He also saw seashells, fossil trees, oceanic islands, and coral reefs. On the Galápagos Islands, off South America, he studied finches, tortoises, and more.

Back in England in 1836, Charles's specimens attracted much interest, and the finches were declared to be, in fact, 12 different species. Within months he wrote: "One species does change into another." This, in 1858, became his theory of evolution by natural selection. It was published in *On the Origin of Species* in 1859 after much worry on Charles's behalf. His theory supported science, not "Divine Design," so Charles's reputation was at stake. He expected and received much criticism.

Charles's work challenged established ideas and religious and conservative authorities, but he lived long enough to see his theories gain acceptance. He was awarded the Royal Society's highly esteemed Copley Medal. He died of heart disease and was buried in Westminster Abbey, London, along with monarchs, national figures, and, of course, scientists like Isaac Newton.

Charles Darwin

"A man who dares to waste one hour of time has not discovered the value of life."

Reinhold Messner

Born: September 17, 1944, Brixen, South Tyrol, Italy

Reinhold's father, Josef, was a teacher. He guided his son to his first summit at the age of five. Reinhold had eight brothers and one sister.

When Reinhold was 13, he began climbing with his brother Günther. By the time the brothers were in their early 20s, they were among Europe's best climbers. Reinhold was one of the first and most enthusiastic supporters of alpine mountaineering. In this, climbers carry everything they need—food, shelter, and equipment—for an ascent. Reinhold thought expedition-style mountaineering (where stocked support camps are set up on the route) was "disrespectful" toward nature and mountains.

The brothers' first major Himalayan ascent was the unclimbed Rupal face of Nanga Parbat, the ninth highest mountain in the world. They reached the summit in June 1970, alpine-style and with minimal equipment. But during the descent Günther disappeared in an avalanche and Reinhold lost seven toes and several fingertips to frostbite. Günther's body remained undiscovered until 2005.

Reinhold and Austrian mountaineer, Peter Habeler, gained a reputation for speed. Their 10-hour ascent of the perilous North Face of the Eiger, Switzerland, was unbeaten for 34 years!

Reinhold promoted the cause of ascending Mount Everest without supplementary oxygen even though doctors and experts declared it could not be done. But in 1978, he and Peter became the first to achieve Everest's summit without bottled oxygen. He repeated the feat in 1980, but this time solo— a first—and did the return trek in just four days.

By 1986, Reinhold had become the first to climb the world's 14 peaks with summits in the "death zone," or above 26,000 feet (8,000 m). He did these without bottled oxygen. But there was another challenge: the Seven Summits—to climb the highest peak in each of the seven continents. He was the fifth to complete it. Reinhold was also the first to cross Antarctica and Greenland on skis.

Reinhold has written over 60 books, served as a Green Party representative, and set up a foundation to protect mountains. But closest to his heart are the Messner Mountain Museums, extraordinary buildings that lay bare mountaineering history, the culture of mountain people, and his love of both.

"The wonderful things in life are the things you do, not the things you have."

Isabella Bird

Born: October 15, 1831, Boroughbridge Hall, Yorkshire, U.K.
Died: October 7, 1904, Edinburgh, Scotland, U.K.

Isabella Bird was an English traveler who made a series of remarkable journeys. During her childhood, she suffered from several ailments, and in her 20s, had an operation to remove a tumor from her spine. The operation was not a complete success and left Isabella with insomnia and depression. Her doctors recommended that she travel. In 1854, her father, Reverend Bird, gave her $132 (£100), which funded her trip to North America. The letters she wrote home became the basis for her first book: *The Englishwoman in America*.

In 1858, Reverend Bird died, and the family moved to Edinburgh. Isabella continued to travel, and after some time in Australia she headed to Hawaii in 1872. This six-month stay was a turning point: she taught herself to ride astride a horse (side-saddle was too painful), climbed the island's volcanic peaks, and discovered a passion for visiting remote regions and peoples. Her time in Hawaii was published in *Six Months in the Sandwich Islands*. She then headed to San Francisco, California, and traveled alone by horse to Lake Tahoe, the Rocky Mountains, and Colorado. When caught in a blizzard, her eyelids froze shut, but she kept going and spent several months snowed in at a cabin. Her next adventure was to Japan. There, she stayed among the non-Japanese Ainu tribe on Hokkaido before travelling through Asia to Malaysia.

On her return to Edinburgh in 1850, Isabella discovered that her books had made her famous. Events over the next five years changed Isabella's outlook. The death of her sister was soon followed by Isabella's marriage to John Bishop, and then John's death left her a wealthy woman. She decided to use this money for good purposes, and in Srinigar, India, established the John Bishop Memorial Hospital. From here she traveled to Tibet, northern Iran, Kurdistan, and Turkey. She publicly condemned the cruelty being inflicted on certain Eurasian peoples.

Her next trip took her to Japan, Korea (she was forced to leave when war broke out), and China. Named a "foreign devil" in China, her house was set on fire, and in the mountains near Tibet, Isabella was stoned and knocked unconscious.

On her return from Morocco, Africa, Isabella died. The first female fellow of The Royal Geographical Society was buried in Dean Cemetery, Edinburgh.

Isabella Bird

"A traveller must buy his own experience, and success or failure depends mainly on personal idiosyncrasies."

Fanny Bullock Workman

Born: January 8, 1859, Worcester, Massachusetts, U.S.
Died: January 22, 1925, Cannes, France

Fanny was born into a wealthy family and had been educated by private governesses or at a finishing school. A trip to Europe in 1879 gave her a taste for adventure! Three years after her return to the U.S., Fanny married William Workman. He introduced his wife to mountain climbing, and Fanny became more than competent and enjoyed being a "new American woman." This concept promoted the idea that females could be both athletic and domestic. Fanny was certainly an athlete and a feminist, but not a homemaker.

Fanny continued to climb after having her first child, Rachel. In 1889, William retired and the family moved to Germany where Siegfried was born. Fanny was not a traditional wife and mother, and the children were left in the care of nurses while she and William traveled. In 1893, Siegfried died. At this point, Fanny pursued adventures and a career writing and speaking about them.

By the time Rachel turned 18, her parents had racked up three bike tours. Between 1888 and 1893, they did short expeditions in parts of Europe, and Fanny became one of the first women to climb Mont Blanc, the Jungfrau, and the Matterhorn in the Alps. Their first extended bicycle tour was 2,800 miles (4,500 km) through Spain. They carried 20 pounds (9 kg) of luggage apiece and slept anywhere, even on the roadside. In tours across North Africa and Indochina, Fanny carried a revolver and whip! After cycling across India in 1897 to the Himalayas, they trekked. It was on a 1906 trek that Fanny climbed Pinnacle Peak, setting a women's altitude record that held until 1934.

In 1911, Fanny was the architect of the Workmans' most significant expedition—an exploration of the Siachen Glacier in the Himalayas. They mapped the region, took scientific measurements, and recorded the effects of high altitude on the body.

Fanny earned many medals of honor, was the second woman to address The Royal Geographical Society in London and the first American woman to lecture at the Sorbonne in Paris. She promoted a version of women that rejected Victorian norms, supported equal rights for women, and believed that women were the equal of men. But above all, Fanny wanted to be known as a mountaineer. On her headstone, which is shared with William, it says: "Pioneer Himalayan Explorers."

"...it behoves women, for the benefit of their sex, to put what they do, at least, on record."

John Franklin

Born: April 16, 1786, Spilsby, Lincolnshire, U.K.
Died: June 11, 1847, near King William Island, British Arctic (now Nunavut territory, Canada)

John entered the Royal Navy at age 14, and he accompanied Captain Matthew Flinders on his 1801–1803 circumnavigation of Australia. Later, he served in the Battles of Trafalgar and New Orleans. His first Arctic experience came in 1818 when he was lieutenant on the HMS *Trent* on an expedition to reach the North Pole.

On his first overland expedition (1819–1822), John's mission was to map the north coast of Canada. The team's canoes fared badly so the expedition headed inland. Low on supplies (eating their leather shoes at one point) and after fatal meetings with native tribes, only nine of the 20-strong team survived. John was praised for his handling of this ill-fated expedition. John's second exploration was more successful. He mapped over 1,000 miles (1,600 km) of the Arctic coast. In 1829, John was knighted and appointed governor of Van Diemen's Land (now Tasmania) in Australia.

Two years after returning to England, John was put in command of the Northwest Passage (a seaway linking the Atlantic and Pacific Oceans) expedition. The HMS *Erebus* and HMS *Terror* set off in 1845 to plot this 311 mile (500 km) seaway winding its way between the Arctic and Canadian coast. Two months into their expedition the vessels were sighted by whalers north of Baffin Island. This was the last recorded sighting.

From 1847 to 1880, 39 missions tried to find the explorers or solve the mystery. Evidence of a camp had been found, but in 1859 the seamen's fate was revealed when a note was found. It stated that the ships became trapped in ice in September 1846 off King William Island and that John had died in 1847. In April 1848, 105 survivors headed on foot for the Back River. Inuit hunters told a search party that the men died as they walked. Later examination of discovered skeletons found knife cuts on the bones, indicating that the crew resorted to cannibalism. But the ultimate killers were lead poisoning (lead was used to seal the canned foods on the ship), scurvy, starvation, and disease.

The Northwest Passage expedition cost the lives of 129 men, but John was hailed a hero at the time. Statues and places named in his honor abound. In 2014 and 2016, wrecks of the *Erebus* and *Terror* were found off King William Island. The world remains fascinated by John's ill-fated expedition.

John Franklin

"Not here: The white north has thy bones; and thou, heroic sailor-soul, art passing on thine happier voyage now toward no earthly pole."

—on Sir John Franklin's monument in Westminster Abbey

Benjamin "Pap" Singleton

Born: 1809, Nashville, Tennessee, U.S.
Died: February 17, 1900, Kansas City, Missouri, U.S.

Benjamin was born into slavery, the son of a white father and an enslaved black mother. As a youth, he trained as a carpenter and became very skilled, but Benjamin's biggest regret was that he never learned to read and write.

In 1846, he escaped to freedom and headed north to Canada, but made his home in Detroit, Michigan. There, he became a noted abolitionist (against slavery) and spokesman for African American civil rights. He ran a lodging house for fugitive slaves. After slavery was abolished in 1865, Benjamin returned to Tennessee, but soon realized that black people would never achieve economic equality unless they owned a means, like a farm or business, of earning an independent living.

His attempts to buy land in racially-discriminating and violent Tennessee failed, so between 1877 and 1879, Benjamin, named the "Black Moses," organized an exodus. The first emigration of 200 black Americans to Cherokee County in Kansas was marred by a mining boom that had sent land prices soaring. But the movement of black colonists continued, and Kansas, with its "Free Soil" and anti-slavery stance, was a good destination.

It is estimated that Benjamin and Columbus Johnson, an associate, engineered the resettlement of 20,000–50,000 Exodusters via their Edgewood Real Estate and Homestead Association. Successful communities were eventually established in Kansas, Missouri, Indiana, and Illinois. Some white Americans objected to the arrival of so many poor blacks, but Benjamin stepped up to defend the Exodusters' rights.

In 1880, Benjamin appeared before the U.S. Senate in Washington, D.C., to defend the "Great Exodus." When southern senators tried to discredit his work, his testimony won the day.

In 1881, "Pap" used his reputation to form Colored United Links (CUL). Its goal was to combine the financial resources of all black people to build black-owned businesses. When CUL failed, he encouraged those of African descent to return to their homelands. He strongly felt that black Americans would never succeed in America.

Benjamin retired from activism in poor health. On his death he was buried in an unmarked grave in Union Cemetery, Kansas City.

Benjamin "Pap" Singleton

"Pity for my race caused me to work for them."

Jacques Piccard

Born: July 28, 1922, Brussels, Belgium
Died: November, 1, 2008, La Tour-de-Peilz, Switzerland

Jacques's father, Auguste, was an engineer and adventurer who had, in 1931 and 1932, set altitude records in a hot-air balloon. When Auguste started applying the buoyancy technique of balloons to a deep-sea submersible craft—a bathyscaphe—Jacques joined the endeavor and found his life's work and passion.

Between 1948 and 1955, father and son built three bathyscaphes. One, the *Trieste*, reached a depth of 10,168 feet (3,099 m). This success prompted Jacques to give up his university teaching post, and he headed to America to get funding from the U.S. Navy. At this time the navy were actively looking for underwater salvage, research, and rescue craft. They purchased the *Trieste*, which could now go to depths of 24,000 feet (7,000 m), and hired Jacques as a consultant. He and a U.S. Navy lieutenant, Don Walsh, then planned a daring test for the *Trieste*—a descent to the very deepest point in the ocean floor.

On January 23, 1960, they dived for five hours to a depth of 35,797 feet (10,911 m) and reached Challenger Deep on the floor of the Mariana Trench in the Pacific Ocean. The *Trieste* carried no scientific equipment and no experiments were conducted, but what the two men saw astonished scientists. Over the featureless seabed there were fish and shrimp. Marine biologists disputed this observation and claimed that nothing could survive the immense pressure, which was more than 1,000 times the pressure at sea level. Jacques wrote of the dive in his book, *Seven Miles Down*. Jacques and Don's feat was the first dive to Challenger Deep—there have only been three since!

The next Piccard design was the mesoscaphe *Auguste Piccard* that became the world's first passenger submarine. It was followed by the *Ben Franklin*, a research mesoscaphe with Jacques as mission leader. The mission to study ocean currents lasted for four weeks and covered 1,444 miles (2,324 km). In addition, they studied, for NASA, the effects of extended durations in a confined space.

Jacques formed the Foundation for the Study and Preservation of Seas and Lakes in the 1970s and did his last dive when he was 82. His 1961 prediction that the ocean's depths would be exploited for their resources has become a sad fact. His courage, determination, and ingenuity are Jacques's legacies.

Jacques Piccard

"Here ... was the answer that biologists had asked for the decades. Could life exist in the greatest depths of the ocean? It could!"

Aloha Wanderwell

Born: October 13, 1906, Winnipeg, Canada
Died: June 4, 1996, Newport Beach, California, U.S.

Aloha was born Idris Galcia Hall, and when her father was killed in action in Ypres in June 1917, her mother moved the family to France. Idris was enrolled in a convent school, but she never conformed. Her teachers tried but failed to tame the tomboy in their restless student who dreamed of adventure in exotic places. When she was 16, Idris saw an ad in the *Paris Herald*—"Brains, Beauty & Breeches—World Tour Offer For Lucky Young Woman." Idris applied.

Her application was received by Walter and Nell Wanderwell who had founded a "million-dollar wager endurance race" to circle the globe in Ford Motor Company cars. French-speaking Idris was welcomed to the expedition and nicknamed "Aloha." Team members had to fund themselves on route, and to this end Idris became not just a driver, mechanic, interpreter, and seamstress, but also an actress, photographer, salesperson, and film editor!

Aloha's grueling adventure started in Nice, France, in 1922 and finally ended in 1928. Traveling through Europe, Africa, the Middle East, Asia, and North America, she visited 43 countries, and there was an adventure in every one.

Aloha nearly died of dehydration in the Sudanese desert, disguised herself as a man and prayed in Mecca, camped at the foot of the Great Sphinx, hunted elephants, earned the trust of Chinese bandits, and braved food riots in Germany. Romance also flourished and Aloha and Walter (divorced from Nell) married in 1925 and had two children.

By 1929, the global adventure was over and they released their documentary: *With Car and Camera Around the World*. The Wanderwells became internationally acclaimed. Their next expedition was to South America. Flying a seaplane, Aloha landed on an uncharted part of the Amazon, and recorded a meeting with a then unknown tribe.

In 1932 and on board their yacht, *Carma*, off California, Walter was shot and killed by an unknown assailant. His murder remains unsolved.

Aloha remarried in 1933 and continued traveling, writing, lecturing, and broadcasting. By the end of her life she had visited 80 countries and driven 500,000 miles (804,000 km), all in Fords. The ashes of the "first female to drive around the world" were scattered, as befits a person with wanderlust.

Aloha Wanderwell

"We were off! The whole world was out there. I reaching for it, the world reaching for me—ecstasy— the ravishing thrill."

Annie Londonderry

Born: January 17, 1870, Latvia, Europe
Died: 1947, New York City, New York, U.S.

Annie Cohen's family emigrated to Boston, Massachusetts, when Annie was five. By the time she was 17, both her parents had died. A year later, Annie married Simon Kopchovsky, a peddler and devout Orthodox Jew. Annie sold advertising space and raised their three children.

In 1894, at the height of the bicycle craze that provided women with cheap, affordable transport, two rich Boston men made a bet. They wagered $20,000 against $10,000 that no woman could bicycle around the world in 15 months and earn $5,000 while she did it. The wager was to test female endurance, wit, and independence.

Annie Kopchovsky was an unlikely choice. She was a Jew in an anti-Semitic country, of small stature and light build, and had first ridden a bike only a few days earlier! But, Annie had *chutzpah*: brazen nerve, boundless self-confidence, and charisma.

She talked Londonderry Lithia Spring Water into a $100 sponsorship. In return, she displayed a company placard and changed her surname to Londonderry. Annie used her salesmanship to get more sponsors and sell merchandise, and her gift of gab to present lectures and demonstrations and get media coverage. She presented herself as a new woman who could do anything a man could do.

On June 27, 1894, Annie set off on her 42 pound (19 kg) Columbia bike from Boston. Wearing a long skirt, corset, and high-collared jacket, and carrying a pearl-handled pistol, she headed off. Using popular cycling routes she arrived in Chicago four months later and 20 pounds (9 kg) lighter. There, she swapped her bike for a lighter men's model, and her skirt for a men's riding suit.

Annie cycled back to New York and caught a ship to France. From Paris, she went by bike and train to Marseilles, then by sea to Japan. At each port, she would do bike trips. In March 1895, Annie sailed into San Francisco and then rode to Los Angeles, where she was nearly killed by a runaway horse. For the next six months she crossed the country, reaching Chicago and the $10,000 prize on September 12, 1895—14 days short of 15 months.

Annie became a journalist, and after rewriting the rules for women and what they could achieve, she spent her final years quietly, with her family.

Annie Londonderry

"What Annie accomplished with her bicycle in 1894–1895 was a tour de force."

—Peter Zheutlin, *Around the World on Two Wheels*

Daniel Boone

Born: November 2, 1734, Reading, Pennsylvania, U.S.
Died: September, 26, 1820, Defiance, Missouri, U.S.

Daniel was born in a log cabin, the sixth of 11 children, to Quaker parents, Squire and Sarah. Daniel's father taught him wilderness survival skills and a relative taught him to read and write.

Daniel worked on the farm. He cared for the cattle, taking them out to graze. He loved being in the outdoors, and at the age of 12 had a rifle and became an expert marksman. Daniel shot much of what the family ate. When Daniel was 15 the family moved to North Carolina. There, Daniel started his own hunting business.

In 1755, Daniel the joined British forces in their fight against the French and Native Americans over territory. When ambushed, Daniel's survival skills saved his life. Within a year he would marry. He was content for many years hunting and providing for his family. But in 1769, Daniel agreed to join a trip to Kentucky. To explore the American frontier had been his childhood dream.

To reach Kentucky, they had to cross the Appalachian Mountains—something few white men dared to do. On reaching Kentucky's wilderness, the men spent several months hunting

and exploring. But they and their deerskins were captured by Shawnee Native Americans. Once again, Daniel managed to escape. He arrived back in North Carolina in 1771, empty-handed.

In 1755, Daniel was hired to cut a road to Kentucky and build a settlement—Boonesborough. Daniel's family joined him. Within a year, Native Americans kidnapped some settlers, including one of Daniel's daughters. Daniel led a successful rescue party, but friction continued and in 1778 Daniel was captured. His hunting skills impressed the chief and Daniel was "adopted" by the tribe. He remained with them for four months. After being robbed of the settlement's money, the Boones fled and moved to Missouri. Daniel continued hunting and became a local administrator. He would settle disputes between local people under the "Judgement Tree."

After the death of his wife, Daniel went back to Kentucky to repay the stolen money. He lived with his children until he died. Two decades later, his body was reburied in Kentucky. Lord Byron's poem about Daniel, *Don Juan*, made Daniel famous, and the legend of this explorer and adventurer turned the woodsman into a symbol of the American frontier.

Daniel Boone

"All you need for happiness is a good gun, a good horse, and a good wife."

Heinrich Barth

Born: February 16, 1821, Hamburg, Germany
Died: November 25, 1865, Berlin, Germany

Heinrich was the third child of Johann Christoph and Charlotte Karoline. Johann had built up a successful trading business, and both parents were orthodox Lutherans who expected their children to conform to their strict ideas of morality. Heinrich excelled at languages and could speak Spanish, Italian, English, and Arabic. On leaving school, he went to university to study classical antiquity.

His first journeys were around the Mediterranean, and then in 1850 he joined an expedition to central West Africa. The expedition's role was to open trade relations on behalf of the British government. Both of his expedition companions died on route, but stalwart and hardy Heinrich continued on alone. He finally reached the ancient city of Timbuktu, now in Mali. Reinhold remained there for six months before heading to London in 1855 via Tripoli in Libya, northern Africa.

Heinrich's feat was astonishing, coming only 28 years after Alexander Gordon Laing became the first European to find the "lost city." For 19th century explorers, Timbuktu was the ultimate prize. The journey cost Laing his life. He was strangled by Tuareg raiders within days of leaving Timbuktu.

The young German's five-year, 10,000 mile (16,000 km) journey through Islamic Africa enlightened the West about the peoples and cultures of the "Dark Continent" as it was then known. His five-volume account of the expedition, *Travels and Discoveries in North and Central Africa*, solved a mystery that had puzzled earlier explorers. It explained how Timbuktu—once the intellectual and spiritual center for Islam and an important trading center in the 15th and 16th centuries—fell into decline when its scholars were expelled and other trade routes were opened.

Heinrich's books were comprehensive. The 3,500 pages covered anthropological (the study of people), historical, and language information, and gave details of his daily travel. At the time, his work was considered the finest of its kind. Naturalist Charles Darwin praised it, and Heinrich was awarded honors and given a financial reward by the British government. Later travels took him to Turkey, Asia Minor, Spain, Italy, and the Alps.

Heinrich died aged 44 and was the first true scholar to visit West Africa, but his scholarship and doggedness are barely remembered today.

Heinrich Barth

"In the river of life he is a bold and persevering swimmer, but not a very agile one."
—Heinrich Barth's brother-in-law

Nellie Bly

Born: May 5, 1864, Cochran's Mills, Pennsylvania, U.S.
Died: January 27, 1922, New York City, New York, U.S.

Nellie was born in a town named for her father, Judge Michael Cochran. When Nellie was six, her father died, which presented the family with a financial problem: he left no will. Her mother remarried, but it was an abusive relationship. A divorce and further hard times followed. These hard times meant that Nellie had little schooling.

After a move to Pittsburgh, Nellie and her mother ran a boarding house. In 1885, Nellie read a story, "What Girls Are Good For" in the *Pittsburgh Dispatch*. Her angry letter to the editor in response to this insulting piece, which described the working woman as a "monstrosity," so impressed the editor he offered Nellie a job.

In her stories for the *Dispatch*, Nellie Bly (her pen name) emphasized women's rights. Her stories covered wider issues—a far cry from the pieces on the "women's pages." Nellie became known for her undercover reporting, once traveling through Mexico to expose official corruption.

In 1887, Nellie moved to New York City. There, she began working for the *New York World*. Her earliest assignment was on patients in a mental institution on Roosevelt Island. Nellie pretended to be insane and was committed for 10 days. Her piece shed light on the staff's physical abuse of the patients, which prompted an investigation, changes to how such places were operated, and increased funding. Nellie's series was reprinted in 1887 as a book, *Ten Days in a Mad House*.

Nellie continued investigative work inside jails and sweatshops. Already famous, Nellie got star status in 1889 when she aimed to beat Jules Verne's fictional Phileas Fogg's *Around the World in Eighty Days* "record." Heading east from New York, she traveled by ship, horse, rickshaw, and sampan to complete the trip in just over 72 days.

In 1895, she married millionaire Robert Seaman, and on his death Nellie took over the running of his business. There, she instigated reforms like healthcare for the staff. The cost of benefits and fraud broke the company, so she went back to journalism. She became America's first female war correspondent for the five years of World War One.

On her death from pneumonia, *The Evening Journal* declared her: "The Best Reporter in America."

Nellie Bly

"I said I could and I would. And I did."

More Explorers & Pioneers

The men and women in this book are a small selection of the many intrepid adventurers there have been throughout history. Their achievements have determined human settlement, thrown light on different cultures, been a testament to human endurance, or changed hearts and minds. Here are some more noteworthy explorers and pioneers:

Thomas Cavendish

Born: September 19, 1560, Suffolk, U.K.
Died: May 1592, onboard *Desire*, North Atlantic Ocean

Thomas was a navigator and pirate who became the third person to circumnavigate the globe, and the first to do it deliberately. On July 21, 1586, he, a crew of 123, and three ships left England, and headed west. When sailing north up America's Pacific coast, they attacked Spanish settlements and ships. The plunder of the *Santa Anna* yielded an immense treasure. Thomas died during his second pirateering circumnavigation.

Jeanne Baret

Born: July 27, 1740, La Comelle, France
Died: August 5, 1807, Saint-Aulaye, France

Jeanne was the first woman to circumnavigate the globe, but it was not planned and she did it dressed as a young man named Jean, pretending to be her botanist boyfriend's assistant. When Jeanne boarded the *Etoile* in 1766, it was for a botanical expedition, and she was dressed as a male as it was illegal to have a female on a French naval vessel. Jeanne was not a botanist, but she worked hard, collected and cataloged specimens, and even named a vine, the Bougainvillea, after the ship's captain. Her disguise went undetected until Tahiti in the Pacific Ocean. Jeanne and her boyfriend were forced off the ship in Mauritius in the Indian Ocean. He died there, and Jeanne finally completed her circumnavigation by returning to France sometime in 1775.

William Beebe

Born: July 29, 1877, Brooklyn, New York, U.S.
Died: June 4, 1962, Simla Research Station, Trinidad

This biologist, explorer, and natural historian was also the co-inventor of the Bathysphere—a spherical steel ball with portholes that was lowered into the ocean by a cable attached to a ship. William and engineer Otis Barton made their first Bathysphere dives in 1930 to a depth of 1,300 feet (400 m). Within a few years, they could go to 3,000 feet (900 m) and the risks were high. If the cable snapped, it meant death. But the rewards for science were great. It was the first time a biologist could observe marine life in its natural habitat. In doing this, William had founded ecology—the study of the interaction among organisms and their environment.

George Everest

Born: July 4, 1790, Powis, Wales, U.K.
Died: December 1, 1866, London, England

After studying at the Military Academy in Woolwich, London, George sailed for India. His math and geometry skills made him perfectly qualified for the Great Trigonometrical Survey of India, the jewel of the British Empire. The survey took 25 years and George was eventually made Surveyor-General. It was his predecessor, Andrew Waugh, who had determined Everest's height during the survey and suggested that the world's tallest mountain be named Everest in honor of George's work.

Louis Antoine, Comte de Bougainville

Born: November 11 or 12, 1729, Paris, France
Died: August 31, 1811, Paris, France

Between 1766 and 1769 Louis commanded France's first circumnavigation of the globe, navigating waters previously unexplored. But there was more to this intelligent man. When French settlers were expelled from areas of America by the British in 1763, Louis financed and commanded the ships for their relocation to the Isles Malouines (later the Falklands) in the Atlantic.

Sylvia Earle

Born: August 30, 1935, Gibbstown, Greenwich Township, New Jersey, U.S.

Her upbringing on a small farm gave Sylvia a respect for nature, and when her family moved to Florida she studied salt marches and seagrass beds. A life devoted to researching algae—from single-celled organisms to forests of kelp in our oceans—had started. In 1970, Sylvia lead a scientists-in-the-sea program. She and other women aquanauts spent up to 20 days in an underwater laboratory studying marine ecology. She then recorded a women's depth dive record (1,250 ft/381 m) in an atmospheric diving suit. Appointed as the first female chief scientist at NOAA and later as explorer-in-residence on National Geographic, she earned the nickname: "Her Deepness." In addition to designing and operating deep-ocean equipment, Sylvia is an expert on the impact of oil spills and her Mission Blue foundation campaigns to protect Earth's oceans.

Zheng He

Born: 1371, Yunnan, China
Died: 1433, Calicut (now Kozhikode), India

Between 1405 and 1433, Zheng He led seven voyages of discovery throughout the Indian Ocean—a surprising event for a Muslim child born in the foothills of the Himalayas! When the Chinese army invaded Yunnan, his father was killed and Zheng He was castrated and sent to serve in the household of the emperor's son in Beijing. Zheng He achieved great status and was made responsible for the building of 3,500 ships. One had nine masts and was 400 feet (121 m) in length. As an admiral, Zheng He's expeditions explored the Indian Ocean and promoted the Chinese dynasty. From East Africa, he returned to China with giraffes and zebras as gifts for the emperor.

Ibn Battuta

Born: February 25, 1304, Tangier, Morocco
Died: 1368–1369, Morocco

At the age of 22, Abu Abdullah Muhammad Ibn Battuta left Tangiers to make a holy pilgrimage to Mecca. After reaching Mecca, Ibn Battuta kept going and covered 73,000 miles (117,000 km) over the next 30 years. He journeyed all over the Islamic world from West Africa through the Indian subcontinent to Southeast Asia and China. His accounts describe societies and their customs, and geography, history, and politics. Ibn Battuta was the greatest traveler of premodern times.